Quick Study

Science

PEARSON
Scott Foresman

Editorial Offices: Glenview, Illinois • Parsippany, New Jersey • New York, New York
Sales Offices: Needham, Massachusetts • Duluth, Georgia • Glenview, Illinois
Coppell, Texas • Sacramento, California • Mesa, Arizona

www.sfsuccessnet.com

Series Authors

Dr. Timothy Cooney
Professor of Earth Science and Science Education
University of Northern Iowa (UNI)
Cedar Falls, Iowa

Dr. Jim Cummins
Professor
Department of Curriculum, Teaching, and Learning
The University of Toronto
Toronto, Canada

Dr. James Flood
Distinguished Professor of Literacy and Language
School of Teacher Education
San Diego State University
San Diego, California

Barbara Kay Foots, M.Ed.
Science Education Consultant
Houston, Texas

Dr. M. Jenice Goldston
Associate Professor of Science Education
Department of Elementary Education Programs
University of Alabama
Tuscaloosa, Alabama

Dr. Shirley Gholston Key
Associate Professor of Science Education
Instruction and Curriculum Leadership Department
College of Education
University of Memphis
Memphis, Tennessee

Dr. Diane Lapp
Distinguished Professor of Reading and Language Arts in Teacher Education
San Diego State University
San Diego, California

Sheryl A. Mercier
Classroom Teacher
Dunlap Elementary School
Dunlap, California

Dr. Karen L. Ostlund
UTeach, College of Natural Sciences
The University of Texas at Austin
Austin, Texas

Dr. Nancy Romance
Professor of Science Education & Principal Investigator
NSF/IERI Science IDEAS Project
Charles E. Schmidt College of Science
Florida Atlantic University
Boca Raton, Florida

Dr. William Tate
Chair and Professor of Education and Applied Statistics
Department of Education
Washington University
St. Louis, Missouri

Dr. Kathryn C. Thornton
Professor
School of Engineering and Applied Science
University of Virginia
Charlottesville, Virginia

Dr. Leon Ukens
Professor of Science Education
Department of Physics, Astronomy, and Geosciences
Towson University
Towson, Maryland

Steve Weinberg
Consultant
Connecticut Center for Advanced Technology
East Hartford, Connecticut

Consulting Author

Dr. Michael P. Klentschy
Superintendent
El Centro Elementary School District
El Centro, California

ISBN: 0-328-14574-2

8 9 10 V031 13 12 11 10 09 08 07

Unit A
Life Science

Unit C
Physical Science

Chapter 12 • Earth and Space

Chapter 13 • Technology in Our World

Name ______________________________

Use with pp. 7–9

Lesson 1: What are the parts of a plant?

Vocabulary

nutrients materials, such as minerals, that living things need to live and grow

roots parts of a plant that hold the plant in place and that take in water and nutrients from the soil

stem part of a plant that holds it up and that carries water and nutrients to the leaves

leaves parts of a plant that use sunlight, air, nutrients, and water to make food for the plant

flower the part of a plant that makes seeds

Plant Parts

A plant has parts to help it get food, water, air, and sunlight. The four main parts of a plant are the roots, stem, leaves, and flowers. Some plants get **nutrients** from water and soil.

Roots grow into the soil. They take water and nutrients from the soil and carry them to the stem. The **stem** carries water and nutrients to the leaves. **Leaves** take in sunlight and air. They use air, sunlight, water, and nutrients to make food.

Many plants have flowers. A **flower** makes seeds. The seeds might grow into new plants.

Name ________________________

Use with pp. 7–9

Lesson 1 Checkpoint

1. What are the four main parts of a plant? Draw a plant. Label the four main parts of the plant.

Use with pp. 10–11

Lesson 2: How are seeds scattered?

Many plants grow from seeds. You scatter seeds in the soil when you plant a garden. Scatter means to spread out. Seeds have room to grow when they are spread out.

Fruits cover and protect seeds. Sometimes air or water scatters fruit. Animals can scatter fruit when it sticks to their fur. Seeds scatter when fruit travels. Scattering helps seeds grow in new places.

The maple tree has fruit. They are shaped like wings. This shape helps the fruit travel through the air. The fruit might land in a place with space, sunlight, water, and good soil. Then, the seed might begin to grow. Over time, it might grow into a tree.

Name ______________________________

Use with pp. 10–11

Lesson 2 Checkpoint

1. Name 3 ways that seeds travel.

Sometimes ____________ or ____________ scatters fruit.

____________ can scatter fruit when it sticks to their fur.

2. **Predict** A maple tree fruit spins to the ground. It lands in an open space. What do you think might happen next?

Draw a box around the paragraph that tells about the maple tree and its fruit.

Name ______________________________

Use with pp. 12–15

Lesson 3: How are plants grouped?

There are two groups of plants. One group has flowers. The other group does not have flowers.

Trees are plants. Some trees have flowers. Peach trees grow flowers. The flowers turn into fruit. The fruit covers the seed inside it. You can eat the fruit of a peach tree.

Plants Without Flowers

Some plants do not have flowers. A pine tree does not have flowers. It has cones. Seeds grow inside the cones. The seeds fall on the ground when the cone opens. Some of these seeds grow into new pine trees.

Mosses are tiny plants. They do not have flowers. They do not make seeds or fruit. Mosses do not have leaves. They do not have stems or roots. Mosses usually grow on wet rocks and rotting wood.

Ferns are also plants that do not have flowers. Ferns do not make seeds. Ferns have leaves, roots, and stems. They live in warm, shady, wet places.

Name ________________________________

Use with pp. 12–15

Lesson 3 Checkpoint

1. How are plants grouped?

There are ____________ groups of plants.

One group has ______________________.

One group does not have ____________.

2. What grows inside cones?
Circle the answer.

flowers seeds fruit

Name ______________________________

Use with pp. 16–19

Lesson 4: How are some woodland plants adapted?

Vocabulary

environment all the things that surround a living thing
adapted changed

A plant's **environment** is all the living and nonliving things around it. Living things have **adapted,** or changed, to live in their environments.

Many plants grow in a woodland environment. A pine tree is adapted to live in cold weather. Its leaves are hard and waxy. This keeps the leaves from drying out.

A maple tree is adapted to live where summers are warm and winters are cold. Maple trees have big, flat leaves. The maple tree loses its leaves in winter to help it keep the water it needs to live.

Plants That Live Near Water

Some plants in a woodland environment live near rivers and streams. They are adapted to live in wet places. The fanwort is a plant that lives in wet places. It has leaves that are adapted to let water move through them.

Name ______________________________

Use with pp. 16–19

Lesson 4 Checkpoint

1. How are pine trees adapted to their environment?

What kinds of leaves does the pine tree have? Circle the answer.

big, flat leaves   hard and waxy leaves

2. How is a fanwort adapted to its wet habitat?

The fanwort has ____________ that are

adapted to let ____________ move through them.

Use with pp. 20–21

Lesson 5: How are some prairie plants adapted?

Vocabulary

prairie flat land covered with grasses and having few trees

Many kinds of plants live in a prairie environment. A **prairie** is a place with lots of grass and few trees. Many prairies have hot summers with little rain. Plants need water to live. Some plants are adapted to keep water when there is not enough rain.

Goldenrod is a prairie plant. The goldenrod has stems and leaves that protect the plant from the Sun. This helps the goldenrod keep water.

Prairie smoke is another prairie plant. It has fuzz on its stems and leaves. The fuzz traps air. The air helps the plant to keep water.

Prairie grass is a prairie plant. It has narrow leaves. The leaves help prairie grass to keep water.

Name ______________________________

Use with pp. 20–21

Lesson 5 Checkpoint

1. How are the stems of goldenrod and prairie smoke alike?

Goldenrod stems protect the plant from the Sun.

This helps the plant to ____________________

____________________________________.

The fuzzy prairie smoke stems trap air.

This helps the plant to ____________________

____________________________________.

Use with pp. 22–23

Lesson 6: How are some desert plants adapted?

Many deserts are hot and sunny during the day. But deserts can be cool at night. Deserts do not get much rain.

Many kinds of plants grow in the desert. Some desert plants are adapted to hold water for a long time. Cactus is a desert plant. Some cactus have stems that hold water.

The desert almond is adapted to hold water. It has leaves that grow in different directions. Some leaves get more sunlight. Leaves that get less sunlight can keep water longer.

Name ___________________________________

Use with pp. 22–23

Lesson 6 Checkpoint

1. Tell about the leaves of a desert almond.

Circle the paragraph that tells about the desert almond.

Use with pp. 24–25

Lesson 7: How are some marsh plants adapted?

A marsh is a very wet place. Many kinds of plants grow in a marsh environment. All plants need nutrients to live and grow. Nutrients are materials that living things need to live and grow. Marsh soil does not have many nutrients. Marsh plants are adapted to get nutrients in other ways.

A cattail is a marsh plant. Cattails are adapted to grow in soil that has a lot of water. Cattails get nutrients from the water.

A sundew is a marsh plant. It has sticky hairs on each leaf. Insects land on the plant. The insects stick to the hairs. Sundews use the insects for nutrients.

A Venus's-flytrap is a marsh plant. It has leaves that trap insects. It gets nutrients from these insects.

Name ______________________________

Use with pp. 24–25

Lesson 7 Checkpoint

1. How does a sundew plant trap insects?

What does the sundew plant have on its leaves?

____

Name ______________________

Use with pp. 39–41

Lesson 1: What are some animals with backbones?

Vocabulary

mammal an animal with bones that usually has hair or fur on its body and feeds milk to its young
bird an animal with a backbone that has feathers, two legs, and wings
fish an animal with bones and gills, and lives in water
reptile an animal with bones that has dry, scaly skin
amphibian an animal with bones that lives part of its life on land and part of its life in water

Groups of Animals with Bones

Bones give an animal shape, help an animal move, and protect the body parts of an animal. **Mammals** have bones and usually hair or fur. Young mammals get milk from their mother. **Birds** are animals with bones, feathers, and wings. Baby birds hatch from eggs. **Fish** are animals with bones. Most fish are covered with scales and live in water. Fish have fins to swim. Fish hatch from eggs. **Reptiles** are animals with bones and scales on their bodies. Some reptiles hatch from eggs. **Amphibians** are animals with bones. They live in water and on land. Most have smooth, wet skin. They hatch from eggs.

Name ______________________________

Lesson 1 Checkpoint

Use with pp. 39–41

Lesson 1 Checkpoint

1. [illegible] kinds of animals have backbones and [illegible]?

____

____

____

____

____

2.  How are an amphibian and a reptile **ali**[illegible] and **different**?

Ho[illegible] are they alike?

____

____

How are they different?

____

____

Name ________________________________

Use with pp. 42–43

Lesson 2: What are some ways mammals are adapted?

Vocabulary

camouflage a color or shape that makes an animal hard to see

Mammals live almost everywhere in the world. Mammals adapt, or change, to live in different environments. An environment is where an animal lives. All the living and nonliving things are part of an animal's environment.

Look at the pictures of the mule deer on page 42 of your textbook. The mule deer adapts to its environment by the use of **camouflage**. Camouflage is a color or shape that makes an animal hard to see. The mule deer's fur is brown in summer. In winter, the mule deer's fur turns gray. This makes it harder for other animals to see the mule deer in the snow.

Some animals change the way they act. Chipmunks save some of the food they find in the summer. They sleep for part of the winter. Every time chipmunks wake up, they eat some of the food they saved.

Name ________________________________

Lesson 2 Checkpoint

Use with pp. 42–43

Lesson 2 Checkpoint

1. How does a mule deer's fur change in winter?

What color is the deer's fur in summer? What color is it in the winter? How does this color help the mule deer in winter?

____

____

____

____

____

Name ______________________

Use with pp. 44–45

Lesson 3: What are some ways birds are adapted?

Birds are adapted to their environment. Most birds use their wings and feathers to fly. The nightjar is a bird that lives in the forest. Its feathers look like the forest floor. This camouflage helps it hide from animals that might eat it.

A hummingbird uses its beak to drink liquid from flowers. Its beak is long and thin. The hummingbird's beak is adapted to help it get food.

Penguins live in very cold places. A penguin's top feathers are waterproof. Tiny feathers below the top layer trap air. The trapped air helps keep the penguin warm. Penguins do not fly. Their wings are adapted for swimming.

Lesson 3 Checkpoint

1. How does camouflage protect the nightjar?

What do the feathers of the nightjar look like? Does the color of the feathers make it easier or harder for the nightjar to hide?

____

____

2. How are hummingbirds and penguins **alike?** How are they **different?**

Talk about the shape of the penguin's wings. Talk about the shape of the hummingbird's beak. How do both these adaptations help the birds?

____

____

____

____

Name ______________________________

Use with pp. 46–47

Lesson 4: What are some ways fish are adapted?

Vocabulary

gills special body parts of some animals that get oxygen from water

Fish are adapted to live in the water. Fish have **gills.** Gills are body parts that help fish breathe in the water. Fish also have fins to help them swim.

The porcupine fish is adapted to protect itself. This fish drinks lots of water to make itself big. This makes sharp spikes stick out of its body. Now the porcupine fish has a new shape and size. Other animals do not want to eat it.

Many catfish live in lakes and rivers. Catfish can swim deep in the water where it is dark. They have feelers that look like whiskers. These feelers help catfish find food.

Name ______________________________

Use with pp. 46–47

Lesson 4 Checkpoint

1. How do porcupine fish protect themselves?

What does the porcupine fish drink? How
s shape and size change? What
ens when its shape and size change?

____

____

____

Name ______________________________

Use with pp. 48–49

Lesson 5: What are some ways reptiles are adapted?

Reptiles are adapted to their environment in many ways. A reptile's body is cold when the air is cold. A reptile's body is warm when the air is warm. Reptiles can move quickly when they are warm.

A chameleon has a long tongue. The chameleon has a sticky ball at the end of its tongue. Food sticks to this ball.

Snakes do not use their teeth for chewing. A snake's mouth is adapted to open very wide to allow it to swallow its food whole.

The desert iguana is adapted to live in the hot, sunny desert. Dark colors get hot in the sun. The desert iguana has pale, light skin that helps it stay cool.

Name ________________________________

Use with pp. 48–49

Lesson 5 Checkpoint

1. How is a desert iguana adapted to live in its environment?

   What kind of skin does the desert iguana have? How does this skin help the iguana?

   ____

   ____

   ____

   ____

Name ________________________________

Use with pp. 50–51

Lesson 6: What are some ways amphibians are adapted?

Amphibians are adapted for life in many different environments. Amphibians begin their life in the water. But they change as they grow. Many amphibians move to the land. Most amphibians have smooth, wet skin that helps them live in water and on land.

Some tree frogs have bright red eyes. Other animals want to eat the frogs. The frogs' eyes help scare these animals away.

Toads are also amphibians. They begin life in the water but move to land when they are grown. Toads dig into the ground when it is hot and dry. They can stay in the ground for a long time. Most toads come out of the ground to look for food at night when it rains. Most toads have dry, rough skin.

Name ______________________________

Use with pp. 50–51

Lesson 6 Checkpoint

1. Name one way a toad and a frog are different.

____

____

What kind of animals are toads and frogs?

____

____

Name ________________________________

Use with pp. 52–55

Lesson 7: What are some animals without backbones?

Vocabulary

insect an animal without bones that has three body parts and six legs

Most kinds of animals in the world do not have backbones. **Insects** are animals that do not have bones. Insects have three body parts: the head, the thorax, and the abdomen. Insects have six legs. Most insects have antennae on their heads to help them feel, smell, hear, and taste things.

A diving beetle's hairy legs are adapted for swimming. Honeypot ants store water and food in their abdomens. They share the water and food with other honeypot ants.

Other Animals Without Backbones

An octopus lives in the ocean and does not have bones. It is adapted to find and catch food. It has good eyesight. This helps it find food. An octopus also has suction cups on its arms to help it hold its food.

Spiders are also animals without bones. They have eight legs. They are adapted to spin webs that catch insects to eat.

Name ______________________________

Use with pp. 52–55

Lesson 7 Checkpoint

1. How is the diving beetle adapted to life in water?

What does a diving beetle have on its legs? What do the legs help the beetle to do?

____

____

____

2. Tell how the octopus is adapted to find food.

Can the octopus see well? How does the octopus hold its food?

____

____

____

Use with pp. 71–73

Lesson 1: What do plants and animals need?

Vocabulary

producer a living thing that makes its own food
consumer a living thing that cannot make food, but it eats food

Plants need air, water, sunlight, and space to grow. Most green plants make their own food. They are **producers.**

Animals need air, water, shelter, and space to live. Animals need food too. Animals are **consumers.** A consumer cannot make its own food. Consumers get food from their habitat.

Many different plants and animals live in a habitat. The plants and animals need different things. They depend on each other to meet their needs. Look on page 72 of your textbook. There is a picture of plants and animals together in their habitat.

Big animals need more food, water, and space. They need a big shelter. Small animals usually need less food and water and live in smaller spaces.

When a habitat does not have enough food for all of the animals, some animals might die.

Name ______________________

Use with pp. 71–73

Lesson 1 Checkpoint

1. What do all animals need?
Look at your summary. Find the paragraph that tells what animals need. Draw a box around it. Then write five things animals need.

____

____

____

____

____

2. **Cause and Effect** What might happen if there is not enough food for all the animals in a habitat?
Sometimes a habitat does not have enough food for all of the animals.

When this happens, ______________________

______________________.

Use with pp. 74–77

Lesson 2: How do plants and animals get food in a grassland?

Vocabulary

food chain Plants use sunlight, air, and water to make food. Animals eat the plants for food. Then other animals eat those animals. This is called a food chain.

predator an animal that hunts another animal for food

prey an animal that is hunted for food

food web A food web is made up of the food chains in a habitat.

All living things need food. Most plants make their own food. Some animals eat plants. Other animals eat those animals. This is called a **food chain.** Food chains start with the Sun. Plants use the Sun's energy to make food. Animals get energy from the food they eat.

All food chains have **predators.** The predator catches and eats other animals. The animals that are caught and eaten are called **prey.**

Most habitats have more than one food chain. Together, the food chains make a **food web.** The food web has plants and animals. The plants and animals need each other for energy.

Name ______________________________

Use with pp. 74–77

Lesson 2 Checkpoint

1. Describe a food web.

Most habitats have more than

one ______________________________.

Together, the food chains make a

food ______________________________.

The food web has ____________ and

______________________________.

The plants and animals need each other

for ______________________________.

2. Give an example of a predator and its prey.

____

Name ______________________________

Use with pp. 78–81

Lesson 3: How do plants and animals get food in an ocean?

Many plants and animals live in an ocean. An ocean has food webs and food chains.

Look at pages 78–79 in your book to see a picture of a food chain in an ocean. Kelp are tall plants that grow in an ocean. A kelp plant uses energy from the Sun to make food. An animal called a sea urchin eats the kelp. A sea star eats the sea urchin. A sea otter eats the sea star. The sea otter gets the energy it needs from the sea star.

A Food Web in an Ocean

Look at the food chains on pages 80–81. Some food chains are short. Some food chains are long. Together, all the food chains make a food web.

The kelp plant is part of two food chains. First the kelp uses energy from the Sun to make food. In one food chain, a kelp crab eats the kelp. In another chain, a sea urchin eats the kelp. Then a sea gull eats the sea urchin. Use your finger to follow the different food chains in the web. How many food chains can you trace?

Name ______________________________

Use with pp. 78–81

Lesson 3 Checkpoint

1. Where does a sea otter get energy?
A sea otter gets energy when it eats a

______________________________.

Draw a picture of a sea otter and how it gets energy.

2. What eats kelp in this food web?
Underline the names of two animals that eat the kelp. Then fill in the blanks.

In one chain, a kelp ____________ eats kelp.

In another chain, a sea __________________ eats kelp.

Name ______________________

Use with pp. 82–83

Lesson 4: What can cause a food web to change?

Many things can change a food web. Some changes are not good for the plants and animals in their habitat. The changes might make it hard for some plants and animals to live there. Plants and animals in the food web may be hurt. Some plants and animals might die.

Sometimes people cause a change in the food web. Sometimes ships have accidents and oil from the ship spills into the ocean. The oil covers plants and animals in the ocean. People work to wash the oil off the animals and help clean the water. They work to make the water safe again for the plants and animals that live there.

Look at the pictures on pages 82–83 in your textbook. They show what happened after a ship spilled oil into the ocean.

Name ______________________________

Use with pp. 82–83

Lesson 4 Checkpoint

1. How did people help after the oil spill?
In the summary, underline three things that people do when oil spills into the ocean.
Then complete the sentences below.

People work to ____________ the oil off the animals.

People help ____________ the water.

They help make the water ______________ again for the plants and animals that live there.

2. **Cause and Effect** What is one effect of an oil spill?
Look in the summary to find the sentence that tells what happens after oil from a ship spilled into the ocean.

Circle the sentence.

Use with pp. 84–89

Lesson 5: How do plants and animals help each other?

Sometimes plants and animals help each other. Some animals get shelter from plants. Ants live in acacia plants. But the ants also protect the plant. The ants bite other animals that try to eat the plant.

Some animals get protection from other animals. Cardinal fish live near sea urchins because the sea urchin has sharp spines. These spines protect the cardinal fish.

Some animals need plants and other animals to build nests. A squirrel uses twigs and leaves to make its nest. The squirrel also uses feathers from birds and wool from sheep for its nest.

Animals need each other. Remora fish need sharks. Sharks protect the remora. The remora eats food the shark leaves behind. The remora does not hurt or help the shark.

A bird called an egret sits on top of a rhinoceros and eats flies that might hurt the rhino.

Name ______________________________

Use with pp. 84–89

Lesson 5 Checkpoint

1. How do ants protect an acacia plant?

Ants ____________ other animals that try to eat the acacia plant.

2. What parts from animals does the squirrel use to make its nest?

leaves   wool   twigs   feathers

3. How does a shark help a remora fish? Draw two pictures that show how a shark helps a remora fish.

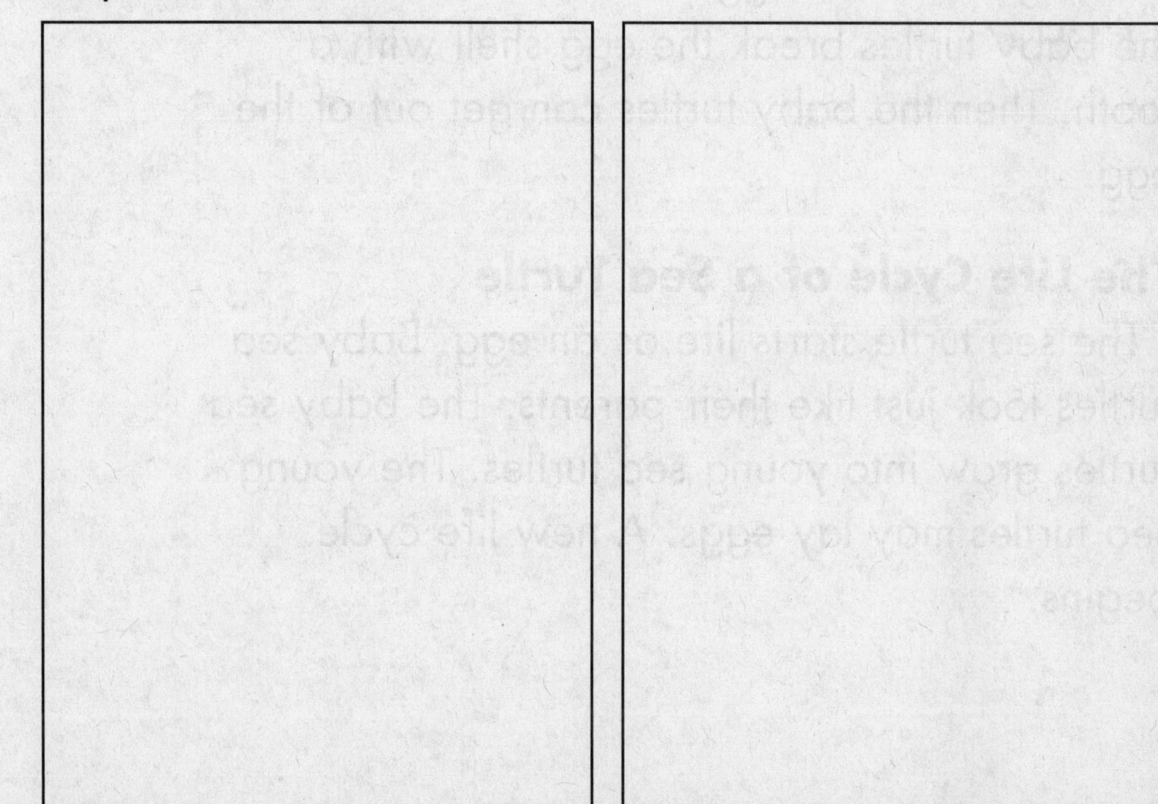

Use with pp. 103–107

Lesson 1: How do sea turtles grow and change?

Vocabulary

life cycle the way a living thing grows and changes

Living things can grow and change. This is called a **life cycle.** A sea turtle is a living thing. It lives in the ocean.

Sea Turtle Eggs

A sea turtle lays eggs in the sand. The baby turtles grow in the eggs. After a few months, the baby turtles break the egg shell with a tooth. Then the baby turtles can get out of the egg.

The Life Cycle of a Sea Turtle

The sea turtle starts life as an egg. Baby sea turtles look just like their parents. The baby sea turtles grow into young sea turtles. The young sea turtles may lay eggs. A new life cycle begins.

Name ______________________________

Use with pp. 103–107

Lesson 1 Checkpoint

1. How do baby sea turtles get out of the egg?
Draw a box around the part of the summary that tells about sea turtle eggs.
Underline the sentence that tells how the baby turtles break the shell.
Then write the missing word in the sentence below.

They break the shell with a __________.

2. How do sea turtles start life?
Write the missing word and draw a picture.

The sea turtle starts life as an ________.

The __________ turtle comes out of the egg.

Name ______________________________

Use with pp. 108–109

Lesson 2: What is the life cycle of a dragonfly?

Vocabulary

nymph a young insect that looks like its parent but has no wings

Insects have a different life cycle than other animals. A dragonfly is an insect. This is a dragonfly's life cycle.

The dragonfly egg hatches.

A **nymph** comes out of the egg. A nymph is a young insect. A nymph looks like its parents but it has no wings. The nymph lives in water. The nymph has an outside covering. The nymph grows. Then the outside covering is too small. The nymph sheds its covering. Now it has a new outside covering. The nymph sheds its covering many times as it grows.

The nymph crawls to the land. It sheds its covering for the last time. It has wings!

The nymph has become a dragonfly. It may lay eggs in the water. Then the life cycle begins again.

Look at the pictures on pages 108–109 in your textbook. They show different parts of the dragonfly's life cycle.

Name ______________________________

Use with pp. 108–109

Lesson 2 Checkpoint

1. Tell the stages of a dragonfly life cycle in order.
These sentences tell about the dragonfly's life cycle. They are not in the right order.
Number the sentences to show what happens first, second, third, and fourth.

_____ A **nymph** comes out of the egg.

_____ The dragonfly egg hatches.

_____ The nymph becomes a dragonfly.
It may lay eggs in the water.

_____ The nymph crawls to the land and sheds its covering for the last time.

2. Infer Why doesn't a nymph need wings?
Look at the summary and draw a box around the part that tells about nymphs.
Underline the sentence that tells where nymphs live.
Then finish the sentence below.

A nymph doesn't need wings because

it ______________________________________.

Name ______________________________

Lesson 3 Summary

Use with pp. 110–111

Lesson 3: What is the life cycle of a horse?

A horse is a mammal. All young mammals grow inside their mothers. After young mammals are born, they drink milk from their mother.

A baby horse is called a foal. When a foal is born it looks like its parents. A foal is smaller than its parents.

The foal drinks milk from its mother. The foal grows and grows. It becomes a young horse.

The young horse eats grass and other things. The young horse grows and grows. It becomes an adult horse. Now the horse is old enough to have foals of its own.

Lesson 3 Checkpoint

1. **Infer** What is food for a foal?
Look at the summary. Find the sentence that tells what happens after a foal is born. Then write the missing words in the sentence.

The foal ____________ ____________

from its mother.

Use with pp. 112–113

Lesson 4: How are young animals like their parents?

Many young animals look like their parents. They are the same shape. They are the same color. But some young animals look different from their parents.

A young penguin looks different. A young penguin has soft fuzzy feathers, but its parents have black and white feathers. Later the young penguin will grow black and white feathers too.

A kitten has the same shape as its parents. Kittens that have the same parents can be different colors.

A young giraffe has the same shape as its parents. It has brown spots like its parents. But the young giraffe's spots look different. Its spots are a lighter brown. The spots are in a different pattern.

Name ______________________________

Use with pp. 112–113

Lesson 4 Checkpoint

1. How are young penguins different from their parents?
Look at the summary. Draw a box around the part that tells about young penguins.
Underline the sentence that tells how the young penguin's feathers are different from its parents' feathers.
Then write the missing words in the sentence below.

A young penguin has ____________

____________ feathers, but its parents have

____________ and ____________ feathers.

Name ______________________

Use with pp. 114–115

Lesson 5: What is the life cycle of a bean plant?

Vocabulary

seed coat the tough outer covering of a seed
germinate to begin to grow into a young plant
seedling a young plant

Most plants grow from seeds.
A seed has a hard cover called a **seed coat.** A seed coat protects the seed.

A seed has a tiny plant and stored food inside it. A seed that gets enough water and air may **germinate.** Germinate means the seed begins to grow. The tiny plant inside it uses the stored food to grow. Roots grow down. A stem grows up. Soon a young plant is growing in the ground. A young plant is called a **seedling.**

The young plant grows and changes. It becomes an adult plant with flowers. The flowers make seeds. Some seeds grow into new plants. The life cycle begins again.

The pictures in your textbook on pages 114–115 show the life cycle of a bean plant.

Name ____________________

Lesson 5 Checkpoint

Use with pp. 114–115

Lesson 5 Checkpoint

1. How does a seed coat help a seed? Look at the summary. Find two sentences that tell about **seed coats.** Circle the sentence that tells what a seed coat does.

Then write the missing word in the sentence.

A seed coat ____________ the seed.

Name ______________________________

Lesson 6 Summary

Use with pp. 116–117

Lesson 6: How are young plants like their parents?

Some young plants are like their parents. They have the same color. They have the same shape. They grow to be the same size.

Some young plants look different from the parent plant. One young cactus plant grows straight and tall. It does not have arms like the parent plant. After many years the young cactus begins to grow arms.

Some people grow flowers called foxgloves. A young foxglove has the same kind of leaves as the parent plant. But a young foxglove is different because it does not have flowers.

When the foxglove is two years old it grows flowers. Foxglove flowers are the same shape. The flowers can be different colors.

Look at your book to see some pictures of a cactus and foxgloves.

Name ______________________________

Use with pp. 116–117

Lesson 6 Checkpoint

1. How are the foxgloves alike and different? Find two paragraphs in the summary that tell about foxglove plants. Draw a box around them. Then write the missing words in the sentences below.

   A young foxglove has the same kind

   of ____________ as the parent plant.

   But a young foxglove is different because it

   does not have ____________.

   Foxglove flowers are the ____________ shape.

   The flowers can be ____________ colors.

   Draw a picture of a young foxglove and an adult foxglove in the space below.

Use with pp. 118–121

Lesson 7: How do people grow and change?

All people are alike in some ways. All people grow and change. First you were a baby. You did not have teeth. You did not talk or walk. You did not read.

You grew. Now you are a child. You have changed in many ways. You will keep growing and changing. You will get taller. You will become a teenager. Later you will be an adult.

Adults do not grow taller, but adults still change. Their skin gets wrinkles. Their hair may turn gray or white.

How People Are Different

People are different in some ways. Some people are short. Some people are tall. People have different eye colors. They have different hair colors. They have different skin colors.

Sometimes children look like their parents. They may have the same shape nose. They might have the same color hair. Sometimes children in a family look like each other. Sometimes they look different.

Look at the family on page 121 of your textbook. How are the children and parents alike? How are they different?

Name ______________________________

Use with pp. 118–121

Lesson 7 Checkpoint

1. What is one way all people are alike? Write the missing words.

All people __________ and __________.

2. What are some ways people grow and change?

Write one way you have changed since you were a baby. __________________

Write one way an adult changes. __________

3. What are some ways people can be different from each other?

Some people are ______________ and some people are ____________.

Some people have ____________ and some people have ____________.

4. **Infer** Look at the picture on page 121 in your textbook. Where did the children in the picture get their dark eyes?

I think the children have dark eyes because

____.

Name ______________________________

Use with pp. 143–145

Lesson 1: What are natural resources?

Vocabulary

natural resource something that people use that comes from Earth

Resources are things people can use. A **natural resource** is a useful material that comes from Earth. Sunlight, water, and trees are natural resources. Oil and coal are too.

Some natural resources can be replaced. People cut down trees. People can plant new trees.

Some natural resources cannot be replaced. Oil and coal are resources that cannot be replaced.

Sunlight, water, and air are natural resources that can never be used up.

Water and Air

Water is a natural resource. Plants, animals, and people need water to live. People drink water and also use it to cook and clean.

Plants, animals, and people need air to live. Air is a natural resource that is all around us. Wind is moving air.

Name ______________________

Use with pp. 143–145

Lesson 1 Checkpoint

1. Name some natural resources.
Draw three natural resources. Write the name of each resource under the picture.

____

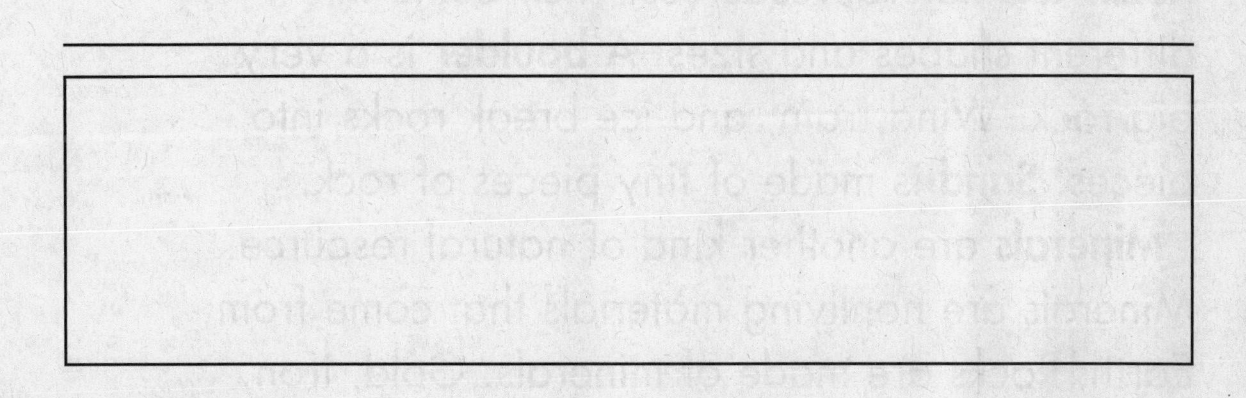

____

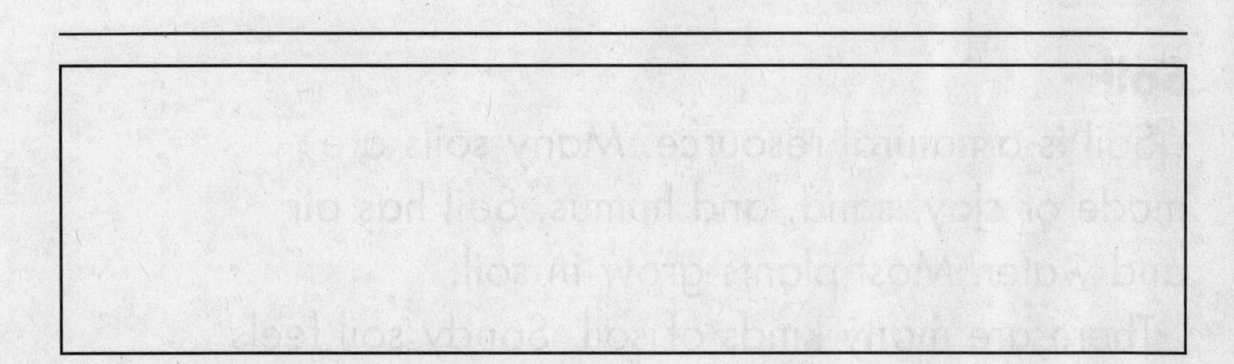

____

Use with pp. 146–149

Lesson 2: What are rocks and soil like?

Vocabulary

boulder a large rock
sand tiny pieces of rock
minerals nonliving solids that come from Earth

Rocks are natural resources. They come in different shapes and sizes. A **boulder** is a very big rock. Wind, rain, and ice break rocks into pieces. **Sand** is made of tiny pieces of rock.

Minerals are another kind of natural resource. Minerals are nonliving materials that come from Earth. Rocks are made of minerals. Gold, iron, silver, and quartz are minerals.

Soil

Soil is a natural resource. Many soils are made of clay, sand, and humus. Soil has air and water. Most plants grow in soil.

There are many kinds of soil. Sandy soil feels dry and rough. Clay soil feels soft and sticky. Humus is the part of soil that comes from living things.

Name ______________________

Use with pp. 146–149

Lesson 2 Checkpoint

1. Name four minerals.

______________ ______________

______________ ______________

2. Describe sandy soil, clay soil, and humus.

____

____

____

3. **Use Picture Clues** Tell how sandy soil, lay soil, and humus are different. Look at ti e pictures on pages 148–149 of your te book.

____

____

____

Name ______________________________

Lesson 3 Summary

Use with pp. 150–151

Lesson 3: How do people use plants?

Plants are natural resources that are used in many ways. Look at the pictures on pages 150–151 in your textbook. The pictures show some of the ways that plants are used.

Cotton comes from a plant. People make clothes from cotton. The shirt is made from cotton.

People use the wood from trees to build houses.

People use wheat to make food. Bread is one of the foods made from wheat.

People also use trees to make paper.

Lesson 3 Checkpoint

1. What is one way that people use cotton plants?
Draw a picture of one thing that is made from cotton.

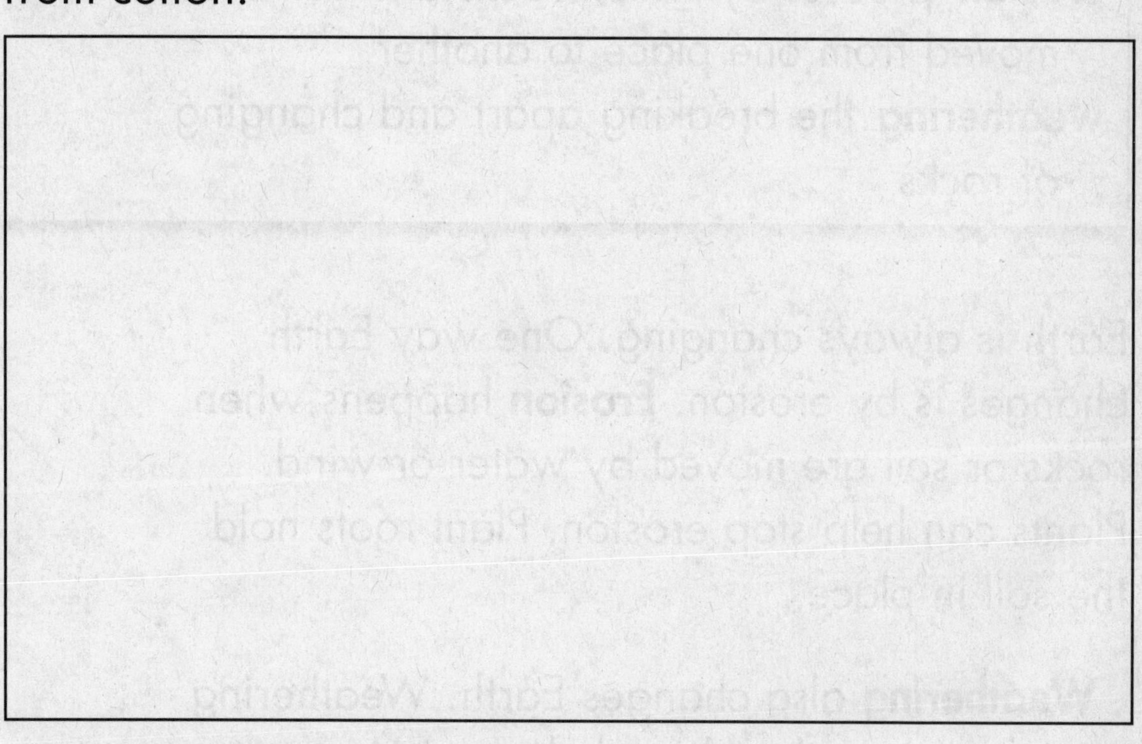

2. **Use Picture Clues** What things are made from trees? Look at the pictures on pages 150–151 of your textbook. Then circle two things below that are made from trees.

houses T-shirts

paper food

Name ______________________________

Use with pp. 152–153

Lesson 4: How does Earth change?

Vocabulary

erosion process by which rocks and soil are moved from one place to another

weathering the breaking apart and changing of rocks

Earth is always changing. One way Earth changes is by erosion. **Erosion** happens when rocks or soil are moved by water or wind. Plants can help stop erosion. Plant roots hold the soil in place.

Weathering also changes Earth. Weathering causes rocks to break and change. Water can cause weathering. Changes in temperature also cause weathering.

Name ______________________________

Lesson 4 Checkpoint

1. How does weathering change Earth?

Weathering causes rocks to ____________

and ______________________________.

Name ______________________________

Use with pp. 154–159

Lesson 5: How can people help protect Earth?

Vocabulary

pollution anything harmful added to land, water, or air
recycle to change something so that it can be used again

People cause **pollution**. Pollution happens when harmful things are added to the land, air, or water. Many people work to reduce pollution. They want to take care of Earth.

People can take care of Earth in many ways. People can pick up litter. Litter is trash on the ground. People can reuse or **recycle** things. This means to use something again. People can recycle cans, glass, paper, plastic, and metal. People can also use less.

People cut down trees and animals that lived in the trees lose their homes. People can help the animals by planting new trees. People build houses on land that plants and animals may have lived on. People can take these plants and animals to a refuge. A refuge is a safe place for plants and animals to live.

Name ______________________________

Use with pp. 154–159

Lesson 5 Checkpoint

1. What is pollution? Look in the summary. Draw a box around the sentence that tells what pollution is.
2. What can you do to help take care of Earth? Draw a picture that shows one way you can help Earth.

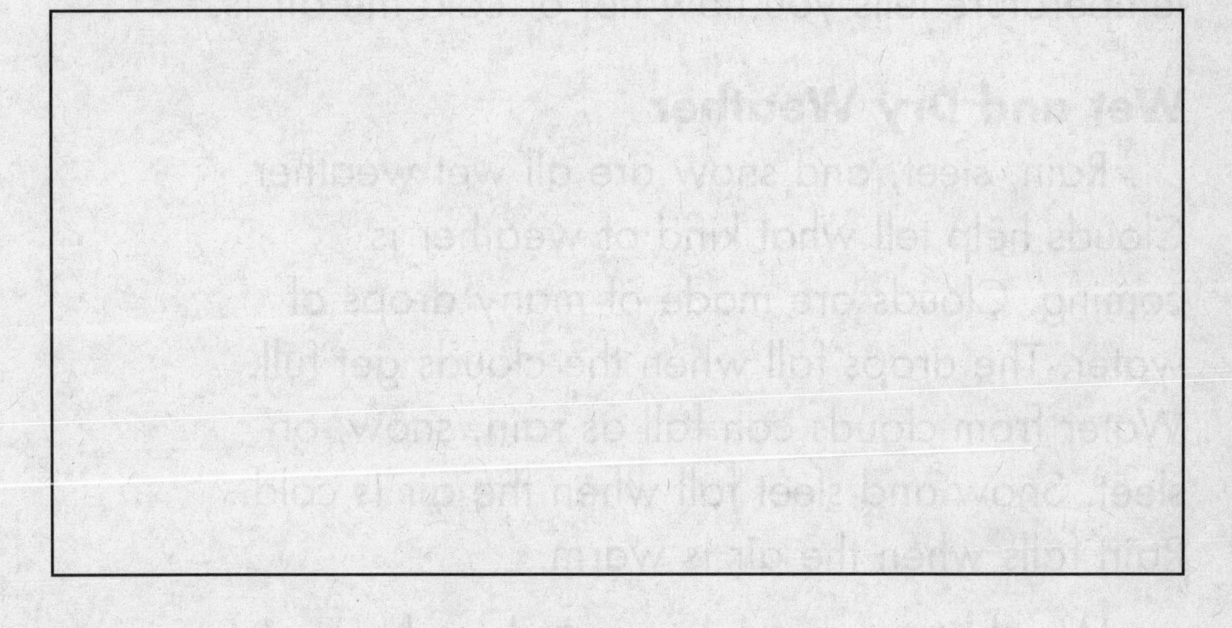

3. What are some ways people can help protect plants and animals?

People can plant new ____________.

People can take plants and animals

to a ____________.

Name ______________________________

Use with pp. 175–177

Lesson 1: What are some kinds of weather?

You wake up in the morning. How do you know what to wear? Check the weather. Is it sunny? Is it raining? Is the wind blowing the trees?

Weather is what the air outside is like. The temperature tells you how hot or cold the air is.

Wet and Dry Weather

Rain, sleet, and snow are all wet weather. Clouds help tell what kind of weather is coming. Clouds are made of many drops of water. The drops fall when the clouds get full. Water from clouds can fall as rain, snow, or sleet. Snow and sleet fall when the air is cold. Rain falls when the air is warm.

Weather can be dry too. A drought can happen when it does not rain for a long time. The land becomes very dry. Plants and animals might not get enough water.

Name ______________________________

Use with pp. 178-179

Lesson 2 Checkpoint

1. What are the steps in the water cycle? Use the word box to complete the sentences.

rivers	water	evaporate	lakes
oceans	clouds	condenses	streams

__________ falls from the clouds. Water flows into __________, __________, and __________. Energy from the Sun makes some of the water __________. Water vapor __________ when it gets cold. These tiny drops of water form __________.

2. **Draw Conclusions** How does energy from the Sun change water in water puddles?

Energy from the Sun makes some of the water __________. The water changes into __________.

Use with pp. 180–181

Lesson 3: What is spring?

What is spring like where you live? In many places, weather changes with the seasons.

There are four seasons in a year. The seasons are spring, summer, fall, and winter.

Some spring days are cool. Other spring days are warm.

Spring days can be rainy. The rain helps plants grow. New leaves start to grow on trees in the spring.

Many animals have babies in the spring.

Name ______________________________

Use with pp. 180–181

Lesson 3 Checkpoint

1. Tell about two things that can happen in spring.
   Complete each sentence below. Draw a picture of each sentence.

Many spring days are ____________.

New leaves start to ____________ on trees.

Name ____________________

Use with pp. 182–183

Lesson 4: What is summer?

What is summer like where you live?

In some places, summer is the hottest season. The days are hot. The nights are warm.

Summer has more daylight hours than spring.

Green leaves grow on many plants and trees. Flowers grow. Fruit and vegetables grow too.

Name ______________________________

Use with pp. 182–183

Lesson 4 Checkpoint

1. How are daylight hours in spring and summer different?
Circle the correct answer.

Summer has **fewer / more** daylight hours than spring.

Name ______________________

Use with pp. 184–185

Lesson 5: What is fall?

Vocabulary

migrate to move from one place to another in a regular pattern

What is fall like where you live? Fall days are shorter than summer days. There are fewer daylight hours. The air temperature begins to get cooler.

The leaves on some trees turn different colors. Then they fall to the ground. Other plants grow more slowly. Farmers pick the crops they grew during the summer.

Some animals collect food for the winter. Squirrels and chipmunks collect food and store it. In the fall, other animals **migrate.** This means they fly to a warmer place where it is easy to find food.

Name ______________________________

Lesson 5 Checkpoint

1. What are two things animals might do in fall?

____

2. **Draw Conclusions** Suppose you see many groups of geese flying south in the fall. What do you think is happening? Complete the conclusion below.

The birds are flying to a ____________ place

where they can ______________________ more easily.

Name ______________________________

Use with pp. 186–187

Lesson 6: What is winter?

Vocabulary

hibernate to spend all winter sleeping or resting

What is winter like where you live? In some places, winter can be very cold. Snow might cover the ground. Ponds and streams may turn to ice.

In winter, there are fewer daylight hours. Winter days are shorter than fall days. In winter, many trees have no leaves. Plants may not grow much.

Some animals **hibernate.** Bears hibernate. This means they have a long, deep sleep. Animals that hibernate wake up in spring. They look for food.

Name ______________________________

Lesson 6 Checkpoint

1. What happens when an animal hibernates?

Bears hibernate. This means they have a long, deep ___________.

Lesson 7: What are some kinds of bad weather?

Vocabulary

lightning a flash of electricity in the sky
tornado very strong wind that comes down from clouds in the shape of a funnel
hurricane a storm that starts over warm ocean waters that has hard rain and very strong winds

A thunderstorm is bad weather with rain, **lightning**, and thunder. Thunder is the sound that comes after lightning.

Tornadoes and Hurricanes

A **tornado** is a very strong wind that can destroy things. Stay safe by going inside a closet or bathroom. Stay away from windows.

A **hurricane** has heavy rains and strong winds. The winds can blow down buildings.

Name ______________________________

Use with pp. 188–193

Lesson 7 Checkpoint

1. What is lightning?

Lightning is a flash of ____________ in the ____________.

2. What is one way to stay safe during a tornado?

Go inside a ____________ or____________.

3. What is a hurricane?

A hurricane is a large ____________ that starts over warm ocean water.

4. **Draw Conclusions** What might happen to objects left outside during a hurricane?

A hurricane has strong __________.

Objects left outside can be ______________ away.

Name ______________________________

Use with pp. 207–209

Lesson 1: How can we learn about the past?

Vocabulary

fossil a part or a print of a plant or animal that lived long ago

paleontologist a scientist who studies fossils

Have you ever seen a fossil? A **fossil** is a print or a part of a plant or an animal that lived long ago. Some fossils are very old bones.

Paleontologists are scientists who study fossils. Paleontologists use fossils to learn what plants and animals looked like long ago.

How Fossils Form

Look at the fossils on pages 208–209 of your textbook. The pictures show how a fossil is made. First, a lizard dies. Then, mud and sand cover the lizard. Finally, the mud and sand turn to rock. The fossil is in the shape of a lizard.

Name ______________________________

Use with pp. 207–209

Lesson 1 Checkpoint

1. What are fossils?

A fossil is the ____________ of a plant or an animal that lived long ago.

A fossil can also be the ____________ of a plant or an animal that lived long ago.

2. **Retell** how fossils are formed. Write the sentences in the boxes in the correct order.

Sand and mud cover the animal.

An animal dies.

The sand and mud become rock.

1.

↓

2.

↓

3.

Name ______________________

Use with pp. 210–211

Lesson 2: What can we learn from fossils?

Vocabulary

extinct an animal or plant no longer living on Earth

Fossils tell us about the past. Fossils show the size of plants and animals from the past. Fossils also show the shape of plants and animals from the past.

Some of these plants and animals are **extinct.** An extinct plant or animal does not live on Earth anymore. Why do some living things become extinct?

Sometimes a habitat cannot meet the needs of the plants and animals that live there. Some plants and animals cannot live when this happens. They may disappear from Earth forever.

Name ______________________________

Use with pp. 210–211

Lesson 2 Checkpoint

1. What do paleontologists learn from fossils?

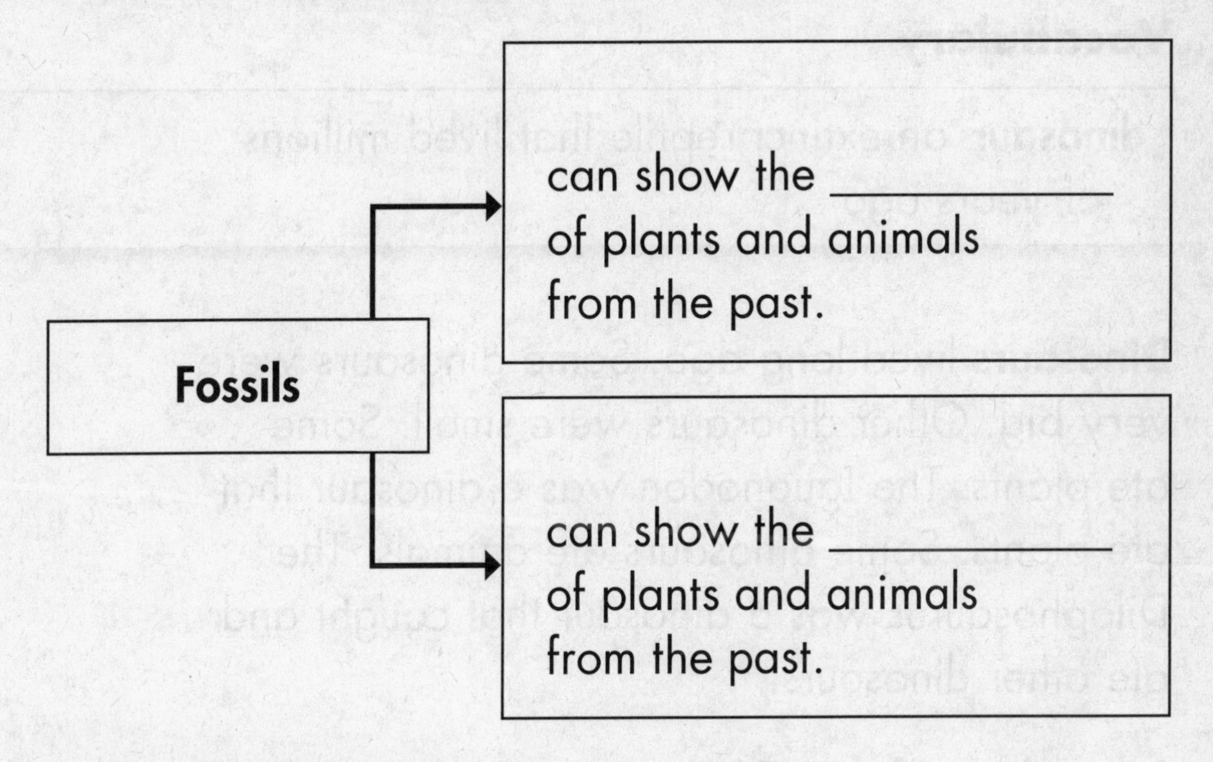

2. **Retell** What can happen to some living things when their habitat no longer meets their needs?

Some plants and animals cannot

__________. They may disappear from

Earth __________.

Name ______________________

Use with pp. 212–215

Lesson 3: What were dinosaurs like?

Vocabulary

dinosaur an extinct reptile that lived millions of years ago

Dinosaurs lived long ago. Some dinosaurs were very big. Other dinosaurs were small. Some ate plants. The Iguanodon was a dinosaur that ate plants. Some dinosaurs ate animals. The Dilophosaurus was a dinosaur that caught and ate other dinosaurs.

Learning About Dinosaurs

Paleontologists study fossils of dinosaur bones. These fossils help scientists learn what dinosaurs looked like. For example, a Compsognathus was as big as a chicken, and the Barosaurus was as tall as a tall building. The Stegosaurus was also a large dinosaur. Its head and mouth were small. Paleontologists think that the Stegosaurus ate plants.

Name ______________________________

Use with pp. 212–215

Lesson 3 Checkpoint

1. What did an Iguanodon eat?

other dinosaurs   plants

2. What did paleontologists learn about a Stegosaurus by looking at its bones?

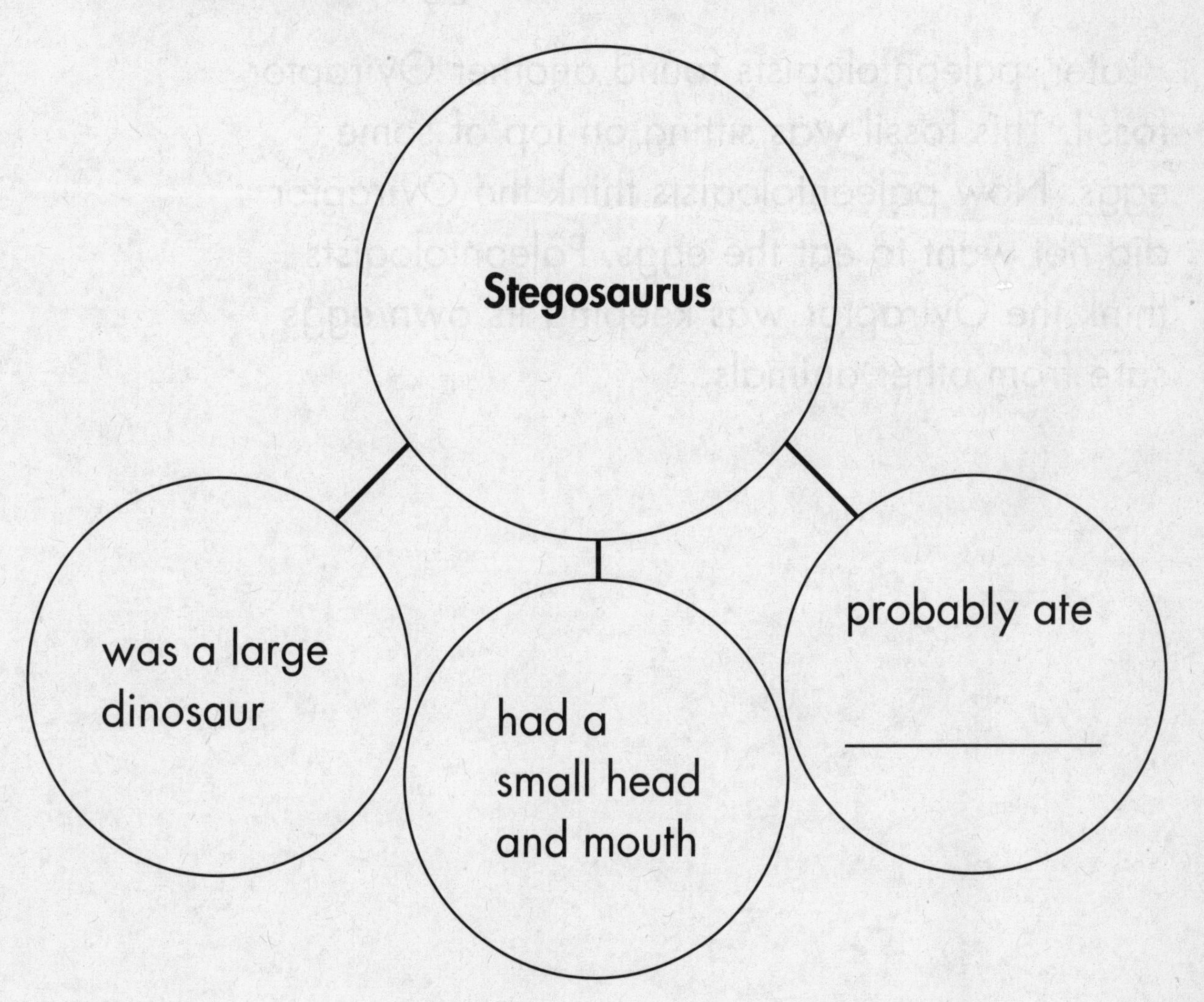

Use with pp. 216–217

Lesson 4: What are some new discoveries?

An Oviraptor was a small dinosaur. Paleontologists found fossils of an Oviraptor near some eggs. Paleontologists thought the Oviraptor was stealing the eggs. Paleontologists thought the Oviraptor was going to eat the eggs.

Later, paleontologists found another Oviraptor fossil. This fossil was sitting on top of some eggs. Now paleontologists think the Oviraptor did not want to eat the eggs. Paleontologists think the Oviraptor was keeping its own eggs safe from other animals.

Name ___________________________

Use with pp. 216–217

Lesson 4 Checkpoint

1. What did paleontologists learn about the Oviraptor?
Circle the correct answer.

The Oviraptor was keeping its eggs safe from other animals.

The Oviraptor wanted to steal eggs to eat them.

Use with pp. 239–241

Lesson 1: What is matter?

Vocabulary

mass how much matter an object has
property something about an object that you can observe with your senses

Look around the classroom. Everything you see is matter. **Matter** is anything that takes up space and has weight. Your desk, the wall, and the books are all matter. Matter is made of very small parts.

Some things you cannot see are also matter. Air is matter.

Anything made of matter has mass. **Mass** is the amount of matter in an object.

Properties of Matter

Can you describe your shoes? To describe your shoes, you use properties. A **property** is something about an object you can observe with your senses. Color, shape, and size are properties. How something feels is a property. How much something weighs is a property. How can you describe the things on your desk?

Name ______________________

Use with pp. 239–241

Lesson 1 Checkpoint

1. What are some properties of matter?

____

____

Circle the properties that describe your pencil.

smooth	hard	bumpy
soft	short	
long	yellow	red
heavy	light	

Name ______________________________

Use with pp. 242–247

Lesson 2: What are the states of matter?

Vocabulary

states of matter three kinds of matter—solids, liquids, and gases

solid matter that has its own shape and takes up space

liquid matter that does not have its own shape

gas matter that always fills the space in a container

The three **states of matter** are solids, liquids, and gases.

A **solid** has its own size and shape. Solids have mass and take up space.

Liquid does not have its own shape. It takes the shape of its container. When you pour water into a glass, it takes the shape of the glass. Liquids have mass and take up space.

Gas takes the size and shape of its container. It always fills up all the space inside its container. It can change size and shape. Gas has mass. It fills up balloons and takes the size and shape of the balloon.

Name ______________________________

Use with pp. 242–247

Lesson 2 Checkpoint

1. What is a solid?

____

____

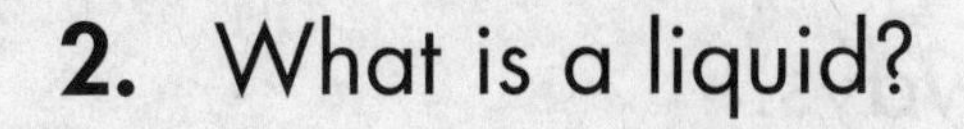

2. What is a liquid?

____

____

3. What are some properties of gases?

____

____

4. **Draw Conclusions** Is there more gas in a full balloon or an empty balloon? Write a sentence to explain your answer.

____

____

Use with pp. 248–251

Lesson 3: How can matter be changed?

Vocabulary

mixture something made up of two or more things that do not change

Matter can be changed in different ways.

You can change the size of matter. You can tear paper into little pieces. You can cut wood into smaller pieces.

You can change the shape of matter. You can fold paper to change its shape. You can mold clay into different shapes.

Mixing and Separating Matter

You can put different matter together. This makes a mixture. A **mixture** is made up of two or more things that do not change. You can make a fruit salad using apples, blueberries, and oranges. To separate the mixture, you can take each kind of fruit out of the salad. Each piece of fruit in the mixture does not change.

Some mixtures are made with water. There are different ways to separate mixtures made with water. You can let the water evaporate. Or you can let the solid matter sink.

Name ______________________________

Use with pp. 248–251

Lesson 3 Checkpoint

1. Name 3 ways that you can change the size or shape of matter.

____

____

____

2. **Draw Conclusions** What might happen to wood if you cut it? How might it change?

____

____

3. What are 2 ways to separate a mixture?

____

____

Lesson 4: How can cooling and heating change matter?

Water is matter. Water can change. It freezes when the temperature is 0° Celsius or lower. When water freezes, it changes from liquid water to a solid—ice.

Water can change from liquid to a gas. This gas is called water vapor. When water vapor touches a cold glass, it turns into a liquid. Tiny drops of water form on the outside of the cold glass.

Heating Matter

Heating can also change the state of matter. Heat can change solids to liquids. Ice and snow melt when the air gets warm. Heat changes the solid ice to liquid water.

Heat also can change liquids to gases. Heat from sunlight changes liquid water in a puddle to a gas, water vapor. This is called evaporation.

When you boil water, the liquid water becomes a gas. It becomes water vapor.

Heat can change other matter from solids to liquids. When you burn a candle, the wax melts.

Name ______________________________

Use with pp. 252–255

Lesson 4 Checkpoint

1. How can you change water from a liquid to a solid?

Water ___________ when the temperature is 0° Celsius or lower.

When water freezes, it changes from

___________ water to a

___________—ice.

2. How can heat change water?

Heat changes the ___________ ice to

___________ water.

When you boil water, the ___________

water becomes a ___________. It becomes

water ___________.

Use with pp. 271–273

Lesson 1: What is energy?

Vocabulary

energy the ability to do work or make changes
solar energy heat and light from the Sun

You use energy all the time. Your body uses energy when you walk, run, and breathe. You use energy when you are awake. You use energy when you sleep. Anything that can do work and cause change has **energy.**

Energy from the Sun

Most energy on Earth comes from the Sun. Heat from the Sun warms the land, air, and water on Earth. **Solar energy** is heat and light from the Sun.

People and animals use sunlight to see during the day. Earth would be dark without the Sun.

Some people use solar energy. Special panels collect solar energy. Solar energy can be used to heat homes.

Name ______________________________

Use with pp. 271–273

Lesson 1 Checkpoint

1. Where does Earth get most of its energy?

Most energy on Earth comes

from ____________.

Lesson 2: How do living things use energy?

Most plants and animals need energy from the Sun. Plants use sunlight, air, and water to make food. Plants use the food to live and grow.

Animals use energy to move, live, and grow. They get energy from food. Some food comes from plants. Other food comes from animals that eat plants.

How People Get Energy

Food gives you energy to work and play. It gives you energy to move and grow. There are five food groups. You should eat food from each group every day to stay strong and healthy. Name something you eat from each food group.

1. Vegetables have many vitamins your body needs.
2. Bread, rice, cereal, and pasta are foods that give you energy.
3. Meat, fish, eggs, and dry beans help your body grow and stay strong.
4. Fruit has many vitamins and minerals that help you stay healthy.
5. Milk, yogurt, and cheese are important for strong bones and teeth.

Name ________________________________

Use with pp. 274–277

Lesson 2 Checkpoint

1. How is energy from the Sun important to plants?

____

____

2. **Infer** How do you think people get and use energy?

____

____

3. Name the five important food groups.

____

____

Name ____________________

Use with pp. 278–281

Lesson 3: What are some sources of heat?

Vocabulary

source a place from which something comes
fuel anything that is burned to make heat or power
conductor something that lets energy flow easily

Sunlight is one source of heat. A **source** is a place from which something comes. Heat comes from different sources.

Fuel is something that is burned to make heat. Wood is fuel. When wood is burned, it makes fire. Fire is a source of heat. Coal, gas, and oil are also fuels.

How Heat Moves

Heat moves from warmer objects and places to cooler ones. A frying pan on a stove gets heat from the hot burner. The heat then moves from the pan to the food.

A frying pan is made of metal, which is a conductor. A **conductor** is something that lets heat move through it easily. Some materials are not good conductors. Wood and cloth are not good conductors. Heat does not move easily through them.

Name ______________________________

Use with pp. 278–281

Lesson 3 Checkpoint

1. What are some sources of heat?

____

____

____

2. Why are many pans made of metal?

____

____

Use with pp. 282–285

Lesson 4: How does light move?

Vocabulary

reflect to bounce back
shadow made when something blocks the light

Light is a form of energy. It can come from the Sun, lamps, and fires. Light moves in straight lines.

Light can move through some things, like clear glass. Light **reflects** when it bounces off something. Light reflects well from smooth, shiny things, like mirrors.

Most light is white light. The colors of the rainbow make up white light. Rainbows form when it rains. Raindrops bend sunlight. Then the sunlight is separated into the different colors of the rainbow. Dark colors take in light. A dark shirt on a sunny day may make you feel warm. Light colors reflect light. You can stay cooler if you wear light colors.

A **shadow** is made when something blocks the light. You can see your shadow when your body blocks the sunlight. Shadows change during the day. They look long when the Sun is low in the sky and short when the Sun looks high in the sky.

Name ______________________

Use with pp. 282–285

Lesson 4 Checkpoint

1. How is a rainbow made?

When do rainbows form? ______________________

What can raindrops do to sunlight?

____

2. Suppose you are standing outside on a sunny day. When would your shadow be the shortest?

____

Name ______________________

Lesson 5 Summary

Use with pp. 286–289

Lesson 5: What are other kinds of energy?

You use different kinds of energy every day. How do you make a toy car move? You can push it. The moving car would have energy of motion.

Have you ever flown a kite? The wind blows it around. Wind is another kind of energy.

Can you name some musical instruments? What kind of sounds do they make? Sound is a kind of energy.

Using Electricity Safely

Electricity is a form of energy. Electricity makes lights work. What other things in your home use electricity?

It is important to use electricity safely. You should follow these tips to help you stay safe.

- Keep things that use electricity away from water.
- Do not put too many plugs into outlets.
- Do not pull on cords to unplug things. Hold onto the plug.
- Do not touch cords that have wires you can see.
- Do not play near power lines.

Name ______________________________

Use with pp. 286–289

Lesson 5 Checkpoint

1. What are some other kinds of energy?

A moving toy car shows energy of ____________.

A kite blowing is an example of ____________ energy.

Making noise with an instrument makes

____________ energy.

2. What is one way you can stay safe around electricity?

____

____

3. **Infer** Why shouldn't you use a hair dryer in the bathroom?

____

____

Name ___________________________

Use with pp. 303–307

Lesson 1: How do objects move?

Vocabulary

motion the act of moving
force a push or pull that makes something move
gravity a force that pulls things toward the center of Earth

Motion is the act of moving. Objects move in different ways. You can push a toy truck in a straight line or in one direction and then another.

Force

A **force** is a push or pull that makes something move in the direction it is pushed or pulled. Pretend your friend kicks a ball to you. The direction of the ball changes when you kick the ball back to your friend.

An object moves faster when you use more force. It also takes more force to move heavier objects than lighter ones.

Gravity

Gravity is a force that pulls things toward the center of Earth. When you throw a basketball into a hoop, gravity pulls it to the ground.

Name ______________________________

Lesson 1 Checkpoint

Use with pp. 303–307

Lesson 1 Checkpoint

1. What is force?
Find the paragraph about force.
Draw a box around the sentence that tells what force is.

2. Why do you come down after you jump up?

__________ pulls you down to Earth.

3. **Put Things in Order** Suppose you wanted to throw a basketball through a hoop. Put the steps you should follow in order. Write the correct number for each step.

__________ Face the basket.

__________ Throw the ball.

__________ Pick up the ball.

Name ______________________________

Use with pp. 308–309

Lesson 2: What is work?

Vocabulary

work when force moves an object

You use force to make objects move. **Work** happens whenever a force makes an object move. You do work when you push a pencil across your desk.

How much work you do depends on how much force you use. It does not take much work to lift a pencil off your desk. How much work you do also depends on how far the object moves. It does take a lot of work to run quickly.

No work is done if an object does not move. Push hard against a wall. Does the wall move? You are not doing any work because the wall does not move.

Use with pp. 308–309

Lesson 2 Checkpoint

1. How can you tell if you are doing work?

Work happens whenever a force makes an

object ___________.

What kind of work do you do? Draw a picture of an example of work you do in the box below.

Lesson 3: How can you change the way things move?

Vocabulary

friction a force that slows down or stops moving objects

It takes more force to move heavier objects than lighter objects. More force is also needed to move objects farther.

Pretend you have a beach ball and a soccer ball. The beach ball is lighter than the soccer ball. It takes more force to kick the soccer ball than the beach ball. You do more work when you use more force.

Friction

Friction is a force. Friction makes moving objects slow down or stop moving. A bicycle moves faster on a smooth road than on grass. There is friction between the tires and the grass. This friction makes the bicycle slow down.

Rub your hands together. How do they feel? Objects get warm when they rub together. Friction causes heat.

Lesson 3 Checkpoint

1. How can the amount of force used change how far an object moves?
Circle the correct word to complete the sentence.

(**More** / **Less**) force is needed to move

objects farther.

2. How does friction change the motion of an object?

Friction makes moving objects ____________

down or ____________ moving.

3. **Put Things in Order** You want to ride your bike. Put the steps you should follow in order. Write the correct number for each step.

____________ Sit on the bike.

____________ Pick up the bike.

____________ Pedal.

Name ______________________

Use with pp. 314–317

Lesson 4: How can simple machines help you do work?

Vocabulary

simple machine a tool with few or no moving parts that makes work easier

A machine is a tool that can do work. A **simple machine** is a tool with few or no moving parts. A machine can make work easier. Some simple machines are listed below.

- A wedge pushes things apart.
- A screw holds things together.
- A lever moves things.
- An inclined plane is higher at one end than the other. An inclined plane makes it easier to move things.
- A wheel and axle work together. The axle turns when you put force on the wheel.
- A pulley is made of a wheel and a rope, and moves an object up, down, or sideways.

Some animal body parts are like simple machines. Animals use their body parts to do work. A beaver has long teeth it uses like a wedge to cut into wood. Some birds have beaks that work like levers to pick berries for food.

Lesson 4 Checkpoint

1. You have to move some heavy boxes. The boxes are on a truck and you want to move them into a store. Which simple machines could you use?

Circle the answers.

wedge lever screw pulley

wheel and axle inclined plane

2. How are a beaver's teeth like a simple machine?

A beaver uses its teeth like a ____________.

Use with pp. 318–321

Lesson 5: What are magnets?

Vocabulary

attract to pull toward
repel to push away

Magnets attract some metal objects. **Attract** means to pull toward. Magnets also repel some metal objects. **Repel** means to push away.

All magnets have a north pole and a south pole. A pole is the place on a magnet that has the strongest push or pull. Magnets repel when you put like poles together. Magnets attract when you put opposite poles together.

What a Magnet Can Attract

Iron and copper are two different kinds of metal. A magnet will attract a nail. Some nails are made of iron. Magnets will not attract a penny. Pennies are made of copper.

Magnets can move some things without touching them. The force of the magnet moves these objects.

Name ______________________________

Use with pp. 318–321

Lesson 5 Checkpoint

1. When do magnets repel each other?

Magnets repel when you put ____________ poles together.

2. What is one kind of metal a magnet will attract?

Circle the name of the object a magnet will attract.

penny nail

What is this object made of? ____________

Name ______________________________

Lesson 1 Summary

Use with pp. 335–337

Lesson 1: What is sound?

Vocabulary

vibrate to move back and forth very fast
loudness how loud or quiet a sound is

Have you heard a band play? Bands have different instruments. Each instrument makes a different sound.

Sound is made when an object vibrates. **Vibrate** means to move quickly back and forth. Instruments make the air vibrate. This makes sounds.

Loudness

Loudness describes sound. **Loudness** means how loud or quiet a sound is.

Pretend you hit a drum very hard. You would make a loud sound.

Pretend you lightly hit a drum. You would make a soft, quiet sound.

Name ______________________________

Use with pp. 335–337

Lesson 1 Checkpoint

1. What does loudness mean?

Loudness means how ____________ or ____________ a sound is.

Read the names of the objects below. Do they make loud or soft sounds? Circle the correct answer.

a bus	loud	soft
turning the page of a book	loud	soft
a baby crying	loud	soft
falling rain	loud	soft

Name ______________________________

Use with pp. 338–339

Lesson 2: What is pitch?

Vocabulary

pitch how high or low a sound is

Pitch is another way to describe sound. **Pitch** means how high or how low a sound is.

Objects that vibrate quickly make a sound with a high pitch. Objects that vibrate slowly make a sound with a low pitch.

Pretend you are blowing across the top of a bottle. This makes the air inside the bottle vibrate. Bottles with a lot of air make sounds with a low pitch. Bottles with a little air make sounds with a high pitch.

Name ______________________________

Use with pp. 338–339

Lesson 2 Checkpoint

1. What does *pitch* mean?
Find the paragraph that tells what pitch means.
Underline the meaning of the word *pitch*.

2. **Important Details** How does the way objects vibrate change pitch?

Objects that vibrate ____________ make a sound with a low pitch.

Objects that vibrate ____________ make a sound with a high pitch.

Name ______________________________

Use with pp. 340–341

Lesson 3: How does sound travel?

Sound moves through solids, liquids, and gases. Sound travels fast though gases, such as air. Your voice travels through air.

Sound travels faster through liquids than through air. Dolphins make sounds in the water. Their sounds move through the water.

Use with pp. 340–341

Lesson 3 Checkpoint

1. Does sound travel faster through air or water?

Sound travels faster through ____________

than ___________.

Use with pp. 342–343

Lesson 4: How do some animals make sounds?

Animals make sounds in many ways. Animals may use parts of their bodies to make sounds.

A cricket makes sounds like a guitar. A cricket rubs one wing on the other wing. This makes the other wing vibrate to make sound.

A rattlesnake makes sounds like maracas. Maracas are like rattles. The snake shakes the rattle in its tail.

A spiny lobster makes sounds like a violin. The lobster rubs its antenna along the side of its head to make sounds.

Name ______________________________

Use with pp. 342–343

Lesson 4 Checkpoint

1. What instrument does a spiny lobster sound like?
   Circle the correct answer.

   guitar violin maracas

2. **Important Details** How does a cricket make sounds?

   The cricket rubs one ____________ on the other ____________ to make sounds.

Name ______________________________

Use with pp. 344–345

Lesson 5: What are some sounds around you?

Listen closely to the sounds around you. What loud sounds can you hear? What soft sounds can you hear?

In your neighborhood, you might hear the siren from a fire truck. You may hear children laughing. You might even hear a fly buzz as it goes by. We hear many loud and soft sounds every day.

Name ______________________________

Lesson 5 Checkpoint

1. What kinds of sounds do you hear in your neighborhood?

Name two soft sounds you hear in your neighborhood.

____

____

Name two loud sounds you hear in your neighborhood.

____

____

Use with pp. 367–369

Lesson 1: What is the Sun?

The Sun is a star. Stars are made of hot, glowing gases. The Sun seems bigger and brighter than other stars. This is because the Sun is the closest star to Earth. The Sun is so bright that you cannot see other stars during the day.

Why We Need the Sun

The Sun looks small because it is far away. But, it is really big. The Sun is much bigger than Earth.

The Sun is important to Earth because Earth gets heat and light from the Sun. Living things on Earth need heat and light. People, plants, and animals can live on Earth because of the Sun.

Name ____________________

Use with pp. 367–369

Lesson 1 Checkpoint

1. Why is the Sun important to living things on Earth? List two things that Earth gets from the Sun.

____

____

2. How are the Sun and other stars **alike** and **different?** Decide whether the words below tell about the Sun, other stars, or both. Then use the words to complete the chart.

closest star to Earth	made of hot, glowing gases
can see at night	can see during the day

Sun	Other Stars

Use with pp. 370–373

Lesson 2: What causes day and night?

Vocabulary

axis an imaginary line around which a planet turns
rotation spinning on an axis

Did you know Earth is always spinning? Look at the picture on page 370 of your textbook. The picture shows a pretend line through the center of Earth. This line is called an **axis**. Earth spins on its axis. This spinning is called a **rotation**. Earth makes one rotation each day.

Earth's rotation causes day and night. Daytime happens when your side of Earth faces the Sun. Nighttime happens when your side of Earth faces away from the Sun.

The Sun in the Sky

The Sun seems to move across the sky during the day. The Sun looks low in the sky early in the morning. It is high in the sky by the middle of the day. The Sun is low in the sky again at night.

The Sun does not really move in the sky. It only looks that way. It is really Earth that is moving.

Use with pp. 370–373

Lesson 2 Checkpoint

1. What is Earth's axis?
Look in the summary and find the paragraph that tells about Earth's axis.

Circle the sentence that tells what Earth's axis is.

2. Why does the Sun look like it is moving across the sky?

The Sun only looks as if it is moving. It is

really the ___________ that is moving.

Use with pp. 374–375

Lesson 3: What causes seasons to change?

Vocabulary

orbit a path around another something

You know that Earth spins on its axis. But did you know that Earth is tilted on its axis? It is always tilted in the same direction.

Earth moves around the Sun, and its path around the Sun is an **orbit**. It takes Earth about one year to orbit the Sun one complete time. The tilt of Earth and Earth's orbit cause the seasons to change.

The four seasons are spring, summer, fall, and winter. When Earth is tilted toward the Sun where we live, we have summer. When the part of Earth where we live is tilted away from the Sun, we have winter.

Name ___________________________________

Use with pp. 374–375

Lesson 3 Checkpoint

1. What causes the seasons to change? Circle the words to answer the question.

Earth's orbit	Earth's axis
Earth's tilt	Earth's rotation

Name ______________________

Use with pp. 376–379

Lesson 4: What can you see in the night sky?

Vocabulary

constellation a group of stars that form a picture
crater a hole that has the shape of a bowl

The Sun is a star you can see during the day. You can see other stars at night.

Long ago, people thought they saw pictures in groups of stars. People pretended that there were lines between the stars. The lines joined to make a picture. A group of stars that make a picture is a **constellation**.

The Moon

You can see the Moon in the night sky too. The Moon is the biggest and brightest object in the night sky.

The Moon has mountains. It also has deep **craters**. A crater is a hole in the ground that is shaped like a bowl. A crater forms when a large rock from space hits the Moon.

Name ______________________________

Use with pp. 376–379

Lesson 4 Checkpoint

1. What is a constellation?
Circle the correct answer below.

A constellation is a group of stars that make a picture.

A constellation is a hole in the ground on the Moon.

2. What causes craters on the Moon?

A crater is formed when a large

____________ from space hits the Moon.

Name ___________________________________

Use with pp. 380–381

Lesson 5: Why does the Moon change?

Vocabulary

phase the shape of the lighted part of the Moon

The Moon rotates just like Earth. The Moon moves in an orbit around Earth. It takes about four weeks for the Moon to move all the way around Earth.

The Moon does not make its own light. But light from the Sun shines on the Moon. You only see the part of the Moon that has light shining on it.

The Moon seems to change shape in the sky. Sometimes the Moon looks round. Sometimes you can only see a small part of the Moon. Sometimes you cannot see the Moon at all. The shape of the lighted part of the Moon is a **phase**.

Name ______________________________

Use with pp. 380–381

Lesson 5 Checkpoint

1. Why can we see the Moon?

Does the Moon make its own light?

yes   no

What shines on the Moon? ____________

Use with pp. 382–383

Lesson 6: What is the solar system?

Vocabulary

solar system the Sun, the planets and their moons, and other objects that orbit the Sun

Earth is a planet. It orbits around the Sun. Other planets orbit around the Sun too. The planets and their moons and other objects that move around the Sun are called the **solar system.**

The Sun is in the middle of our solar system. In our solar system, there are nine planets that move around the Sun. Some planets are closer to the Sun than other planets. Some planets are very big.

Name ______________________________

Use with pp. 382–383

Lesson 6 Checkpoint

1. What is at the center of Earth's solar system? Circle the answer.

the Moon the planets the Sun

2. Look at the planets on pages 382–383 of your textbook. Tell how they are **alike** and **different**.

All of the planets ______________ around the Sun.

Some planets are very ______________.

Name ____________________

Use with pp. 399–401

Lesson 1: What is technology?

Vocabulary

technology how people change nature to meet their needs and wants
invent to make something for the first time
transportation ways to move people or things
engine a machine that changes energy into force or motion

Technology means using science to help us solve problems. People also use technology to invent things. **Invent** means to make something for the first time.

Technology has changed transportation. **Transportation** is the way people or things move from place to place. People can travel farther and faster now than they did long ago.

An **engine** is a machine that makes something move. Steam engines used to make trains and boats move. Today, electric or gasoline engines make cars, trains, and boats move.

Changes in technology help the way people travel. Seat belts and air bags help make cars safer. People also use technology to solve problems. New cars have been invented that use less gasoline. This lowers pollution.

Name ______________________________

Use with pp. 399–401

Lesson 1 Checkpoint

1. How has technology changed transportation? Circle the correct answer.

Transportation is **(faster / slower)** now than it was years ago.

(Steam engines / Gasoline engines) make cars, trains, and boats move.

Seat belts and air bags help make cars **(safer / more dangerous).**

Name ______________________

Use with pp. 402–403

Lesson 2: How does technology help us?

Vocabulary

vaccine medicine that can prevent a disease

Technology can help people stay healthy. Doctors use vaccines to help people stay healthy. A **vaccine** is a medicine that can help prevent a disease.

Doctors can use technology to help people who have trouble seeing and hearing. Glasses and contact lenses can help people who have trouble seeing. Hearing aids help people who have trouble hearing.

Technology helps doctors find out why people are sick. X-rays, CAT scans, and MRIs are tools doctors use to see inside people. Doctors use these tools to find out what is wrong. Then they can help people get well.

Name ______________________________

Use with pp. 402–403

Lesson 2 Checkpoint

1. What are some ways that technology can help people?
Match the technology on the left with its job on the right.

X-rays	help people see.
Glasses	stop people from getting sick.
Vaccines	help doctors find out why people are sick.
Hearing aids	help people hear.

2. **Retell** What are some tools that help doctors see inside people?
Read the last paragraph in the summary.
Write the tools on the lines below.

____

____

____

Use with pp. 404–405

Lesson 3: How do we use technology to communicate?

How do you communicate with your friends? You might make a phone call. You might send an e-mail message from your computer. The way technology is used to communicate has changed over the years.

The first telephones were attached to a wall. Today, telephones are smaller and lighter than they were years ago.

Early computers were very big and heavy and filled a whole room. Very few companies used computers. Today, computers are smaller and lighter. Computers help us communicate with astronauts in space.

Name ______________________________

Use with pp. 404–405

Lesson 3 Checkpoint

1. How has technology changed the way people communicate?
How do you communicate with your friends?
Draw a picture to show one way you use technology to communicate.

Write a sentence about your picture.

____

Name ______________________________

Use with pp. 406–407

Lesson 4: What are some other ways we use technology?

Vocabulary

meteorologist a person who studies weather
satellite an object that revolves around another object

Technology has changed the way people have fun. People listen to music on compact discs and use computers to play games.

Technology can make our lives easier. People use calculators to do math. People use Velcro to close things.

Technology also helps people in their jobs. A **meteorologist** is a person who studies weather. Meteorologists study weather using satellites. A **satellite** is an object that moves around another object. Satellites in space send pictures back to Earth. Meteorologists use the satellite pictures to tell us what the weather will be like.

Name ______________________________

Use with pp. 406–407

Lesson 4 Checkpoint

1. How does a meteorologist use information from satellites?

Satellites in space send ____________ back to Earth.

Meteorologists use this information to tell us

what the ______________ will be like.

Name ______________________

Use with pp. 408–409

Lesson 5: How do people make things?

Vocabulary

manufacture to make by hand or by machine

People manufacture things we use every day. **Manufacture** means to make by hand or by machines.

Different kinds of materials are used to manufacture things. Some materials come from nature. For example, a coat can be made using wool from sheep. The buttons on a coat can be made using wood from a tree.

Some materials are made by people. The tires on a bicycle are made from rubber. Some bicycle seats are made from plastic. Plastic and rubber are materials made by people.

Name ______________________________

Use with pp. 408–409

Lesson 5 Checkpoint

1. What are some manufactured things you use in school?
   Draw and label two manufactured things you use in school.

2. **Retell** What are some materials used to make a bicycle?

   Circle the materials.

   plastic wool rubber

   wood glass